This is a technical explanation of the Protocol signed at Washington on March 8, 2004 (the "Protocol"), amending the Convention between the United States of America and the Kingdom of the Netherlands for the avoidance of double taxation and the prevention of fiscal evasion with respect to taxes on income, signed at Washington on December 18, 1992 (the "1992 Convention"), as amended by a protocol signed at Washington on October 13, 1993 (the "1993 Protocol"). The term "Convention" refers to the 1992 Convention as modified by both the 1993 Protocol and the Protocol.

Negotiations took into account the U.S. Treasury Department's current tax treaty policy and the Treasury Department's Model Income Tax Convention, published on September 20, 1996 (the "U.S. Model"). Negotiations also took into account the Model Tax Convention on Income and on Capital, published by the Organization for Economic Cooperation and Development, as updated in January 2003 (the "OECD Model"), and recent tax treaties concluded by both countries.

The Technical Explanation is an official guide to the Protocol. It reflects the policies behind particular Protocol provisions, as well as understandings reached with respect to the application and interpretation of the Protocol and the 1992 Convention. This Technical Explanation should be read together with the Technical Explanation to the 1992 Convention with respect to provisions that have not been modified.

The Protocol was accompanied by a detailed Understanding, implemented through an exchange of notes, indicating the views of the negotiators and of the States with respect to a number of provisions of the Convention. The Understanding supersedes the Understanding accompanying the 1992 Convention and the related exchange of notes accompanying the 1993 Protocol. The portions of the Understanding that have been added (as opposed to being merely repeated) are discussed in connection with the relevant portions of the Protocol.

Paragraph XXXVIII of the Understanding provides that the United States and the Netherlands will consult together at regular intervals regarding the terms, operation and application of the Convention to ensure that it continues to serve the purposes of avoiding double taxation and preventing fiscal evasion. The first such consultation will take place no later than December 31st of the fifth year following the date on which the Protocol enters into force in accordance with the provisions of Article 10 of the Protocol. Further consultations shall take place thereafter at intervals of no more than five years. The Understanding also provides that the United States and the Netherlands will conclude further protocols to amend the Convention, if appropriate.

References in the Technical Explanation to "he" or "his" should be read to mean "he or she" or "his or her."

Article 1

Article 1 of the Protocol modifies Article 1 (General Scope) of the Convention to add new paragraph 3. Paragraph 3 specifically relates to the application to the Convention of dispute-resolution procedures and non-discrimination provisions under other agreements. The provisions of paragraph 3 are an exception to the rule provided in subparagraph (b) of paragraph 2 of Article 1 under which the Convention shall not restrict in any manner any benefit now or hereafter accorded by any other agreement between the Contracting States.

Clause (i) of subparagraph (a) of paragraph 3 provides that, notwithstanding any other agreement to which the Contracting States may be parties, a dispute concerning the interpretation or application of the Convention, including a dispute concerning whether a measure is within the scope of the Convention, shall be considered only by the competent authorities of the Contracting States, and the procedures under Article 29 (Mutual Agreement Procedure) of the Convention exclusively shall apply to the dispute. Thus, dispute-resolution procedures that may be incorporated into trade, investment, or other agreements between the Contracting States shall not apply in determining the scope of the Convention.

Clause (ii) of subparagraph (a) of paragraph 3 provides that the national treatment provisions of Article XVII of the General Agreement on Trade in Services ("GATS") shall not apply to any "measure" unless the competent authorities agree that such measure is not within the scope of the non-discrimination provisions of Article 28 (Non-Discrimination) of the Convention. Subparagraph (b) of paragraph 3 defines the term "measure" to mean a law, regulation, rule, procedure, decision, administrative action, or any similar provision or action, as related to taxes of every kind and description imposed by a Contracting State. Accordingly, no national treatment obligation undertaken by a Contracting State pursuant to GATS shall apply to a measure, unless the competent authorities agree that it is not within the scope of the Convention. The provision does not provide any limitation on the application of the most favored nation obligation ("MFN") of Article II of GATS. Because there is no MFN obligation in the Convention, there can be no conflict between the Convention and the MFN obligation of GATS.

Unlike the analogous provision in the U.S. Model, paragraph 3 does not include limitations on the application of the national treatment and MFN obligations of other agreements. The U.S. Model provision states generally that national treatment or MFN obligations undertaken by the Contracting States under any agreement other than the tax treaty and the General Agreement on Tariffs and Trade as applicable to trade in goods do not apply to a taxation measure, unless the competent authorities otherwise agree. Except as discussed above with respect to GATS, subparagraph 2(b) of the Convention provides that if there were overlap between Article 28 of the Convention and the national treatment or MFN obligations of any agreement, benefits would be available under both the Convention and that agreement. In the event of such overlap, to the extent benefits are available under that agreement that are not available under Article 28 of the Convention, a resident of a Contracting State is entitled to the benefits provided under the overlapping agreement.

Article 2

Article 2 of the Protocol modifies Article 4 (Resident) of the 1992 Convention by eliminating a special rule regarding the residence of estates and trusts. This rule is no longer necessary as the Protocol adopts a more general rule regarding fiscally transparent entities, found in a new paragraph 4 of Article 24 (Basis of Taxation) of the Convention. The new paragraph is discussed below in the Technical Explanation to Article 6 of the Protocol.

Although the general rule regarding the determination of residence has not been changed, subparagraph (b) of Paragraph I of the Understanding clarifies the application of the existing definition with respect to certain dual resident companies. If a company is a resident of one of the Contracting States under the domestic law of that State, but is treated as a resident of a third state under a treaty between that State and the third state, then it will not be treated as a resident of the Contracting State for purposes of the Convention. For example, if a company that is organized in the Netherlands is managed and controlled in the United Kingdom, both countries would treat the company as being a resident under its domestic laws. However, the treaty between the Netherlands and the United Kingdom assigns residence in such a case to the country in which the company's place of effective management is located. Assuming that, in this case, the place of effective management is the United Kingdom, the company would not qualify for benefits under the U.S.–Netherlands treaty because it is not subject to tax in the Netherlands as a resident of the Netherlands. The paragraph in the Understanding thus is consistent with the holding of Rev. Rul. 2004-76, 2004-31 I.R.B. 111.

Article 3

Paragraph a) of Article 3 of the Protocol replaces Article 10 (Dividends) of the Convention. Article 10 provides rules for the taxation of dividends paid by a company that is a resident of one Contracting State to a beneficial owner that is a resident of the other Contracting State. The Article provides for full residence country taxation of such dividends and a limited source-State right to tax. Finally, the Article prohibits a State from imposing taxes on a company resident in the other Contracting State, other than a branch profits tax, on undistributed earnings.

Paragraph 1

The right of a shareholder's country of residence to tax dividends arising in the source country is preserved by paragraph 1, which permits a Contracting State to tax its residents on dividends paid to them by a company that is a resident of the other Contracting State.

Paragraph 2

The State of source also may tax dividends beneficially owned by a resident of the other State, subject to the limitations of paragraphs 2 and 3. Paragraph 2 generally limits the tax in the State of source on the dividend paid by a company resident in that State to 15 percent of the gross amount of the dividend. If, however, the beneficial owner of the dividend is a company that is a resident of the other State and that directly owns shares representing at least 10 percent of the voting power of the company paying the dividend, then the withholding tax in the State of source is limited to 5 percent of the gross amount of the dividend. Shares are considered voting shares if they provide the power to elect, appoint or replace any person vested with the powers ordinarily exercised by the board of directors of a U.S. corporation.

The benefits of paragraph 2 may be granted at the time of payment by means of reduced withholding at source. It also is consistent with the paragraph for tax to be withheld at the time of payment at full statutory rates, and the treaty benefit to be granted by means of a subsequent refund so long as refund procedures are applied in a reasonable manner.

The term "beneficial owner" is not defined in the Convention, and is, therefore, defined as under the internal law of the country imposing tax (*i.e.*, the source country). The beneficial owner of the dividend for purposes of Article 10 is the person to which the dividend income is attributable for tax purposes under the laws of the source State. Thus, if a dividend paid by a corporation that is a resident of one of the States (as determined under Article 4 (Resident)) is received by a nominee or agent that is a resident of the other State on behalf of a person that is not a resident of that other State, the dividend is not entitled to the benefits of this Article. However, a dividend received by a nominee on behalf of a resident of that other State would be entitled to benefits. These interpretations are confirmed by paragraph 12 of the Commentary to Article 10 of the OECD Model. See also paragraph 24 of the Commentary to Article 1 of the OECD Model.

Companies holding shares through fiscally transparent entities such as partnerships are considered for purposes of this paragraph to hold their proportionate interest in the shares held by the intermediate entity. As a result, companies holding shares through such entities may be able to claim the benefits of subparagraph (a) under certain circumstances. The lower rate applies when the company's proportionate share of the shares held by the intermediate entity meets the 10 percent threshold. Whether this ownership threshold is satisfied may be difficult to determine and often will require an analysis of the partnership or trust agreement.

Paragraph 3

Paragraph 3 provides exclusive residence-country taxation (*i.e.* an elimination of withholding tax) with respect to certain dividends distributed by a company that is a resident of one Contracting State to a resident of the other Contracting State. As described further below, this elimination of withholding tax is available with respect to certain inter-company dividends.

Subparagraph (a) of paragraph 3 provides for the elimination of withholding tax on dividends beneficially owned by a company that has owned directly 80 percent or more of the voting power of the company paying the dividend for the 12-month period ending on the date the dividend is declared.

Eligibility for the elimination of withholding tax provided by subparagraph (a) is subject to additional restrictions based on, but supplementing, the rules of Article 26 (Limitation on Benefits). These restrictions are necessary because of the increased pressure on the Limitation on Benefits tests resulting from the fact that the United States has relatively few treaties that provide for such elimination of withholding tax on inter-company dividends. The additional restrictions are intended to prevent companies from re-organizing in order to become eligible for the elimination of withholding tax in circumstances where the Limitation on Benefits provision does not provide sufficient protection against treaty-shopping.

For example, assume that ThirdCo is a company resident in a third country that does not have a tax treaty with the United States providing for the elimination of withholding tax on inter-company dividends. ThirdCo owns directly 100 percent of the issued and outstanding voting stock of USCo, a U.S. company, and of DCo, a Netherlands company. DCo is a substantial company that manufactures widgets; USCo distributes those widgets in the United States. If ThirdCo contributes to DCo all the stock of USCo, dividends paid by USCo to DCo would qualify for treaty benefits under the active trade or business test of Paragraph 4 of Article 26. However, allowing ThirdCo to qualify for the elimination of withholding tax, which is not available to it under the third state's treaty with the United States (if any), would encourage treaty-shopping.

Accordingly, a company that meets the holding requirements described above still will qualify for the benefits of paragraph 3 only in certain circumstances. Under Article 10(3)(b), publicly-traded companies and subsidiaries of publicly-traded companies will qualify for the elimination of withholding tax without meeting any additional requirements. Thus, a company that is a resident of the Netherlands and that meets the listing and trading requirements of Article 26(2)(c) will be entitled to the elimination of withholding tax, subject to the 12-month holding period requirement of Article 10(3).

In addition, under Article 10(3)(c), a company that is a resident of a Contracting State may also qualify for the elimination of withholding tax on dividends if it satisfies the derivative benefits test of paragraph 3 of Article 26. Thus, a Netherlands company that owns all of the stock of a U.S. corporation can qualify for the elimination of withholding tax if it is wholly-owned, for example, by a U.K. or a Mexican publicly-traded company that otherwise satisfies the requirements to be an "equivalent beneficiary". At this time, ownership by companies that are residents of other EU, EEA or NAFTA countries would not qualify the Netherlands company for benefits under this provision, as the United States does not have treaties that eliminate the withholding tax on inter-company dividends with any other of those countries. If the United States were to negotiate such treaties with more of those countries, residents of those countries could then qualify as equivalent beneficiaries for purposes of this provision.

The derivative benefits test may also provide benefits to U.S. companies receiving dividends from Netherlands subsidiaries, because of the effect of the Parent-Subsidiary Directive in the European Union. Under that directive, inter-company dividends paid within the European Union are free of withholding tax. Under subparagraph (g) of paragraph 8 of Article 26, that directive will also be taken into account in determining whether the owner of a U.S. company receiving dividends from a Netherlands company is an "equivalent beneficiary". Thus, a company that is a resident of a Member State of the European Union will, by definition, meet the requirements regarding equivalent benefits with respect to any dividends received by its U.S. subsidiary from a Netherlands company. For example, assume USCo is a wholly-owned subsidiary of ICo, an Italian publicly-traded company. USCo owns all of the shares of DCo, a Netherlands company. If DCo were to pay dividends directly to ICo, those dividends would be exempt from withholding tax in the Netherlands by reason of the Parent-Subsidiary Directive, even though the tax treaty between Italy and the Netherlands otherwise would allow the Netherlands to impose a withholding tax at the rate of 5 percent. If ICo meets the other conditions of subparagraph 8(f) of Article 26, it will be treated as an equivalent beneficiary by reason of subparagraph 8(g) of that Article.

A company also could qualify for the elimination of withholding tax pursuant to Article 10(3)(c) if it is owned by seven or fewer U.S. or Netherlands residents who fall within a limited category of "qualified persons." This rule would apply, for example, to certain Netherlands corporations that are closely-held by a few Netherlands resident individuals or charities.

The definition of "equivalent beneficiary" is also intended to ensure that certain joint ventures, not just wholly-owned subsidiaries, can qualify for benefits. For example, assume that the United States were to enter into a treaty with Country X, an EU, EEA or NAFTA country, that includes a provision identical to Article 10(3). USCo is 100 percent owned by DCo, a Netherlands company, which in turn is owned 49 percent by PCo, a Netherlands publicly-traded company, and 51 percent by XCo, a publicly-traded company that is resident in Country X. In the absence of a special rule for interpreting derivative benefits provisions, each of the shareholders would be treated as owning only their proportionate share of the shares held by DCo. If that rule were applied in this situation, neither shareholder would be an equivalent beneficiary, since neither would meet the 80 percent ownership test with respect to USCo. However, since both PCo and XCo are residents of countries that have treaties with the United States that provide for elimination of withholding tax on inter-company dividends, it is appropriate to provide benefits to DCo in this case.

Accordingly, the definition of "equivalent beneficiary" includes a rule of application that is intended to ensure that such joint ventures qualify for the benefits of Article 10(3). Under that rule, each of the shareholders is treated as owning shares with the same percentage of voting power as the shares held by DCo for purposes of determining whether it would be entitled to an equivalent rate of withholding tax. This rule is necessary because of the high ownership threshold for qualification for the elimination of withholding tax on inter-company dividends.

A company that qualifies for the benefits of the Convention under a Limitation on Benefits provision other than the rules described above will qualify for the elimination of withholding tax on inter-company dividends only if it acquired shares representing 80 percent or more of the voting stock of the company paying the dividends prior to October 1, 1998, or it receives a determination from the competent authority with respect to Article 10(3). Accordingly, in the first example above, DCo will not qualify for the elimination of withholding tax on dividends unless it owned USCo before October 1, 1998. If it did own USCo before October 1, 1998, then it will continue to qualify for the elimination of withholding tax on dividends so long as it qualifies for benefits under at least one of the tests of Article 26. So, for example, if ThirdCo decides to get out of the widget business and sells its stock in DCo to FWCo, a company that is resident in a country with which the United States does not have a tax treaty, DCo would continue to qualify for the elimination of withholding tax on dividends so long as it continues to meet the requirements of the active trade or business test of Article 26(4) or, possibly, the competent authority discretionary test of Article 26(7).

The result would be different under the "ownership-base erosion" test of Article 26(2)(f). For example, assume DCo is a passive holding company owned by Netherlands individuals, which was established in 1996 to hold the shares of USCo. DCo qualifies for the benefits of the Convention only under the ownership-base erosion test of Article 26(2)(f). If the Netherlands individuals sell their stock in DCo to FWCo, DCo would lose all the benefits accorded to residents of the Netherlands under the Convention (including the elimination of withholding tax on dividends) because the company would no longer qualify for benefits under Article 26 (unless, of course, the U.S. competent authority were to grant benefits under Article 26(7)).

If a company does not qualify for the elimination of withholding tax under any of the foregoing objective tests, it may request a determination from the relevant competent authority pursuant to paragraph 7 of Article 26. Benefits will be granted with respect to an item of income if the competent authority of the Contracting State in which the income arises determines that the establishment, acquisition or maintenance of such resident and the conduct of its operations did not have as one of its principal purposes the obtaining of benefits under the Convention.

In making its determination under Article 26(7) with respect to income arising in the United States, the U.S. competent authority will consider the obligations imposed upon the Netherlands by its membership in the European Communities. In particular, the

United States will have regard to any legal requirements for the facilitation of the free movement of capital among Member States of the European Communities. The competent authority will also consider the differing internal tax systems, tax incentive regimes and tax treaty practices of the relevant Member States.

For example, in the case above where DCo ceased to qualify for the elimination of withholding tax because it was acquired by FWCo, the competent authority would consider whether FWCo were a resident of a Member State of the European Communities. If it were, that would be a factor in favor of a determination that DCo is entitled to the benefits of the elimination of withholding tax on dividends. This would be particularly true if the U.S. business was a relatively small portion of the business acquired. However, that positive factor could be outweighed by negative factors. One negative factor could be a determination by the U.S. competent authority that FWCo benefited from a tax incentive regime that eliminated any domestic taxation. The competent authority would also consider facts that might indicate that an acquisition was not undertaken "under ordinary business conditions" but instead was undertaken to acquire the Netherlands-U.S. "bridge." These might include the fact that the Netherlands company was acquired even though all or substantially all of the business activities acquired consisted of the U.S. business; the fact that existing U.S. operations were restructured in an attempt to benefit from the elimination of withholding tax on dividends; or the fact that FWCo was owned by residents of a country that is not a Member State of the European Communities. Finally, another significant negative factor would be if the U.S. competent authority faced difficulties in learning the identity of FWCo's owners, such as an uncooperative taxpayer or legal barriers such as "economic espionage" or other limitations on the effective exchange of information in the country of which FWCo is a resident.

Paragraph VIII of the Understanding establishes a hierarchy with respect to these tests. Any company that acquired the shares of the paying company after September 30, 1998, may request a discretionary ruling from the competent authority, unless it would qualify for benefits under subparagraphs 3(b) or 3(c). Thus, the competent authority could agree that a company may qualify for the elimination of withholding tax even if it satisfies Limitation on Benefits under the active conduct of a trade or business or the headquarters company test, or even if it does not satisfy any of the objective tests in Article 26. However, the competent authority will not give "comfort rulings" to companies that meet the requirements of another subparagraph of paragraph 3.

Paragraph 4

Paragraph 4 modifies in particular cases the maximum rates of withholding tax at source provided for in paragraphs 2 and 3.

Subparagraph (a) provides that dividends paid by a U.S. Regulated Investment Company ("RIC") or U.S. Real Estate Investment Trust ("REIT") or a Dutch beleggingsinstelling are not eligible for the 5 percent maximum rate of withholding tax in subparagraph (a) of paragraph 2 or the elimination of withholding tax of paragraph 3.

Subparagraph (b) of paragraph 4 provides that the 15 percent maximum rate of withholding tax in subparagraph (b) of paragraph (2) shall apply for dividends paid by a RIC or a Dutch beleggingsinstelling (subject to the rule in subparagraph (c) regarding beleggingsinstellings that invest primarily in real estate).

Subparagraph (c) provides that the 15 percent withholding rate in subparagraph (b) of paragraph (2) shall apply for dividends paid by a REIT or a beleggingsinstelling that invests in real estate to the same extent as a REIT, provided certain conditions are met. First, the dividend may qualify for the 15 percent maximum rate if the person beneficially entitled to the dividend is an individual holding an interest of not more than 25 percent in the REIT or beleggingsinstelling. Second, the dividend may qualify for the 15 percent maximum rate if it is paid with respect to a class of stock that is publicly traded and the person beneficially entitled to the dividend is a person holding an interest of not more than 5 percent of any class of stock of the REIT or beleggingsinstelling. Third, the dividend may qualify for the 15 percent maximum rate if the person beneficially entitled to the dividend holds an interest in the REIT or beleggingsinstelling of 10 percent or less and the REIT or beleggingsinstelling is "diversified" (*i.e.*, the gross value of no single interest in real property held by the REIT or beleggingsinstelling exceeds 10 percent of the gross value of the REIT's or beleggingsinstelling's total interest in real property). For purposes of this diversification test, foreclosure property is not considered an interest in real property, and a REIT or beleggingsinstelling holding a partnership interest is treated as owning its proportionate share of any interest in real property held by the partnership. Finally, the 15 percent rate will apply with respect to dividends paid by a REIT to a beleggingsinstelling or by a beleggingsinstelling to a RIC or REIT.

The restrictions set forth above are intended to prevent the use of these investment vehicles to gain inappropriate source-country tax benefits for certain shareholders resident in the other Contracting State. For example, a company resident in the Netherlands that wishes to hold a diversified portfolio of U.S. corporate shares could hold the portfolio directly and pay a U.S. withholding tax of 15 percent on all of the dividends that it receives. Alternatively, it could hold the same diversified portfolio by purchasing 10 percent or more of the interests in a RIC. If the RIC is a pure conduit, there may be no U.S. tax cost to interposing the RIC in the chain of ownership. Absent the special rule in paragraph 4, such use of the RIC could transform portfolio dividends, taxable in the United States under the Convention at 15 percent, into direct investment dividends subject to no or 5 percent withholding tax.

Similarly, a resident of the Netherlands directly holding U.S. real property would pay U.S. tax either at a 30 percent rate on the gross income or at graduated rates on the net income. As in the preceding example, by placing the real property in a REIT, the investor could transform real estate income into dividend income, taxable at the rates provided in Article 10, significantly reducing the U.S. tax that otherwise would be imposed. Paragraph 4 prevents this result and thereby avoids a disparity between the taxation of direct real estate investments and real estate investments made through REIT conduits. In the cases where the rules provide for a maximum 15 percent rate of withholding tax, the holding in the REIT is not considered the equivalent of a direct holding in the underlying real property.

Paragraph 5

Paragraph 5 clarifies that the restrictions on source country taxation provided by paragraphs 2, 3 and 4 do not affect the taxation of the profits out of which the dividends are paid. The taxation by a Contracting State of the income of its resident companies is governed by the internal law of the Contracting State, subject to the provisions of paragraph 5 of Article 28 (Non-Discrimination).

Paragraph 6

Paragraph 6 provides a broad and flexible definition of the term "dividends." This paragraph has not been amended by the Protocol. The definition is intended to cover all arrangements that yield a return on an equity investment in a corporation as determined under the tax law of the state of source, including types of arrangements that might be developed in the future.

The term dividends includes income from shares, or other corporate rights that are not treated as debt under the law of the source State, that participate in the profits of the company. The term also includes income that is subjected to the same tax treatment as income from shares by the law of the State of source. Thus, a constructive dividend that results from a non-arm's length transaction between a corporation and a related party is a dividend.

In the case of the United States, the term dividends includes amounts treated as a dividend under U.S. law upon the sale or redemption of shares or upon a transfer of shares in a reorganization. See, *e.g.*, Rev. Rul. 92-85, 1992-2 C.B. 69 (sale of foreign subsidiary's stock to U.S. sister company is a deemed dividend to extent of subsidiary's and sister's earnings and profits). Further, a distribution from a U.S. publicly traded limited partnership, which is taxed as a corporation under U.S. law, is a dividend for purposes of Article 10. However, a distribution by a limited liability company is not characterized by the United States as a dividend and, therefore, is not a dividend for purposes of Article 10, provided the limited liability company is not taxable as a corporation under U.S. law.

Finally, a payment denominated as interest that is made by a thinly capitalized corporation may be treated as a dividend to the extent that the debt is recharacterized as equity under the laws of the source State. In the case of the United States, these rules include section 163(j) of the Internal Revenue Code of 1986 (the "Code").

The term dividends also includes, in the case of the Netherlands, income from profit sharing bonds, and, in the case of the United States, income from debt obligations that carry the right to participate in profits.

Paragraph 7

Paragraph 7 provides that the rules of paragraphs 1, 2, 3, and 4 do not apply with respect to dividends paid with respect to holdings that form part of the business property of a permanent establishment or fixed base situated in the source country. Such dividends will be taxed on a net basis using the rates and rules of taxation generally applicable to residents of the State in which the permanent establishment is located, as modified by the Convention. An example of dividends paid with respect to the business property of a permanent establishment would be dividends derived by a dealer in stock or securities from stock or securities that the dealer held for sale to customers. In such a case, Article 7 (Business Profits) applies with respect to business profits from a permanent establishment and Article 15 (Independent Personal Services) applies to income from the performance of personal services in an independent capacity from a fixed base.

In the case of a permanent establishment that once existed in the State but that no longer exists, the provisions of paragraph 7 also apply, by virtue of paragraph 3 of Article 24 (Basis of Taxation), as modified by paragraph (d) of Article 6 of this Protocol, to dividends that would be attributable to such a permanent establishment if it did exist in the year of payment or accrual.

Paragraph 8

A State's right to tax dividends paid by a company that is a resident of the other State is restricted by paragraph 8 to cases in which the dividends are paid to a resident of that State or are attributable to a permanent establishment in that State. Thus, a State may not impose a "secondary" withholding tax on dividends paid by a nonresident company out of earnings and profits from that State. In the case of the United States, paragraph 8, therefore, overrides the ability to impose taxes under sections 871 and 882(a) on dividends paid by foreign corporations that have a U.S. source under section 861(a)(2)(B).

The paragraph also restricts a State's right to impose corporate level taxes on undistributed profits, other than a branch profits tax. The accumulated earnings tax and the personal holding company taxes are taxes covered in Article 2 (Taxes Covered). Accordingly, under the provisions of Article 7 (Business Profits), the United States may not impose those taxes on the income of a resident of the other State except to the extent that income is attributable to a permanent establishment in the United States. Paragraph 8 further confirms the restriction on the U.S. authority to impose those taxes. The paragraph does not restrict a State's right to tax its resident shareholders on undistributed earnings of a corporation resident in the other State. Thus, the U.S. authority to impose the foreign personal holding company tax, its taxes on subpart F income and on an increase in earnings invested in U.S. property, and its tax on income of a passive foreign investment company that is a qualified electing fund is in no way restricted by this provision.

Paragraph (b) of Article 3 provides updated cross-references in Article 25 (Methods of Elimination of Double Taxation).

Relation to Other Articles

Notwithstanding the foregoing limitations on source country taxation of dividends, the saving clause of paragraph 1 of Article 24 (General Scope) permits the United States to tax dividends received by its residents and citizens, subject to the special foreign tax credit rules of paragraph 6 of Article 25 (Methods of Elimination of Double Taxation), as if the Convention had not come into effect.

The benefits of this Article are also subject to the provisions of Article 26 (Limitation on Benefits). Thus, if a resident of the Netherlands is the beneficial owner of dividends paid by a U.S. company, the shareholder must qualify for treaty benefits under at least one of the tests of Article 26 in order to receive the benefits of this Article.

Article 4

Article 4 of the Protocol amends Article 11 (Branch Tax) of the Convention by inserting a new sentence at the end of paragraph 3. Paragraph 1 of Article 11 permits a Contracting State to impose a branch tax on the dividend equivalent amount of a company resident in the other Contracting State which derives business profits attributable to a permanent establishment located in the first-mentioned State or which derives income subject to tax on a net basis in the first-mentioned State under Article 6 (Income from Real Property) or Article 14 (Capital Gains).

Paragraph 3 of Article 11 of the 1992 Convention provides that the branch profits tax will not be imposed at a rate exceeding the five percent rate allowed by paragraph 2(a) of Article 10 (Dividends), ensuring parallel treatment for branches and subsidiaries. The new sentence added to paragraph 3 further ensures such parallel treatment by providing for an exemption from the branch profits tax under conditions that parallel those for the elimination of withholding tax on inter-company dividends. Pursuant to paragraph 3, the branch profits tax may not be imposed in the case of a company which, before October 1, 1998, was engaged in activities giving rise to profits attributable to a permanent establishment (whether or not the permanent establishment was actually profitable during that period) or to income or gains that are of a type that would be subject to the provisions of Article 6 or paragraphs 1 or 4 of Article 13. In addition, the branch profits tax may not be imposed in the case of a company which is a qualified person by reason of subparagraph (c) of paragraph 2 of Article 26 (Limitation on Benefits) (*i.e.*, a publicly-traded company) or a company that would be entitled to benefits with respect to dividends under paragraph 3 of Article 26. Finally, the branch profits tax does not apply to a company that has received a ruling from the competent authority pursuant to paragraph 7 of Article 26 with respect to the dividend equivalent amount.

Thus, for example, if a Netherlands company would be subject to the branch profits tax with respect to profits attributable to a U.S. branch and not reinvested in that branch, paragraph 3 may apply to eliminate the branch profits tax if that branch was established in the United States before October 1, 1998 and the other requirements of the Convention (e.g., Limitation on Benefits) are met. If, by contrast, a Netherlands company that did not have a branch in the United States before October 1, 1998, takes over, after October 1, 1998, the activities of a branch belonging to a third party, then the branch profits tax would apply, unless the Netherlands company is a qualified person under subparagraph (c) of paragraph 2 of Article 26, or is entitled to benefits under paragraph 3, or paragraph 7 of that Article.

Moreover, if a branch that satisfied the requirements of paragraph 3 of Article 11 by reason of having been involved in activities in the other State before October 1, 1998 transfers assets to a newly-incorporated, wholly-owned company, the treaty-shopping concerns described above do not exist. Accordingly, in that case, it is expected that the U.S. competent authority will exercise its discretion to treat the new parent-subsidiary group as qualified for the elimination of withholding tax as well, so long as the Netherlands parent meets the other ownership requirements of paragraph 3 of Article 10 with respect to the subsidiary.

Article 5

Article 5 of the Protocol updates the Convention's rules regarding cross-border pension contributions by eliminating the current rule, found in paragraph 5 of Article 28 (Non-Discrimination) and replacing it with new paragraphs 7 through 11 of Article 19 (Pensions, Annuities, Alimony).

Paragraph 7

New paragraph 7 of Article 19 of the Convention provides that if a resident of a Contracting State is a member or beneficiary of, or a participant in, an exempt pension trust established in the other Contracting State, the State of residence will not tax the income of the exempt pension trust with respect to that resident until a distribution is made. Thus, for example, if a U.S. citizen contributes to a U.S. qualified pension plan while working in the United States and then establishes residence in the Netherlands, paragraph 7 prevents the Netherlands from taxing currently the plan's earnings and accretions with respect to that individual. When the resident receives a distribution from the pension fund, that distribution may be subject to tax in the State of residence, subject to paragraphs 1, 2 and 3 of Article 19 (Pensions, Annuities, Alimony). The paragraph also makes clear that the U.S. citizen will not be subject to tax if he rolls over the balance in one exempt pension trust into another U.S. fund that qualifies as an exempt pension trust.

Paragraph 8

New paragraph 8 of Article 19 of the Convention provides certain benefits with respect to cross-border contributions to an exempt pension trust, subject to the limitations of paragraph 9 of the Article. It is irrelevant for purposes of paragraph 8 whether the participant establishes residence in the State where the individual renders services (the "host State"). The provisions of paragraph 8 are similar to the provisions of the U.S. Model with respect to pension contributions.

Subparagraph (a) of paragraph 8 allows an individual who exercises employment or self-employment in a Contracting State to deduct or exclude from income in that Contracting State contributions made by or on behalf of the individual during the period of employment or self-employment to an exempt pension trust established in the other Contracting State. Thus, for example, if a participant in a U.S. qualified plan goes to work in the Netherlands, the participant may deduct or exclude from income in the Netherlands contributions to the U.S. qualified plan made while the participant works in the Netherlands. Subparagraph (a), however, applies only to the extent of the relief allowed by the host State (*e.g.*, the Netherlands in the example) for contributions to an exempt pension trust established in that State.

Subparagraph (b) of paragraph 8 provides that, in the case of employment, accrued benefits and contributions by or on behalf of the individual's employer, during the period of employment in the host State, will not be treated as taxable income to the employee in that State. Subparagraph (b) also allows the employer a deduction in computing business profits in the host State for contributions to the plan. For example, if a participant in a U.S. qualified plan goes to work in the Netherlands, the participant's employer may deduct from its business profits in the Netherlands contributions to the U.S. qualified plan for the benefit of the employee while the employee renders services in the Netherlands.

As in the case of subparagraph (a), subparagraph (b) applies only to the extent of the relief allowed by the host State for contributions to pension funds established in that State. Therefore, where the United States is the host State, the exclusion of employee contributions from the employee's income under this paragraph is limited to elective contributions not in excess of the amount specified in section 402(g). Deduction of employer contributions is subject to the limitations of sections 415 and 404. The section 404 limitation on deductions is calculated as if the individual were the only employee covered by the plan.

Paragraph 9

Paragraph 9 limits the availability of benefits under paragraph 8. Under subparagraph (a) of paragraph 9, paragraph 8 does not apply to contributions to an exempt pension trust unless the participant already was contributing to the trust, or his employer already was contributing to the trust with respect to that individual, before the individual began exercising employment in the State where the services are performed (the "host State"). This condition would be met if either the employee or the employer was contributing to an exempt pension trust that was replaced by the exempt pension trust to which he is contributing. The rule regarding successor trusts would apply if, for example, the employer has been taken over by a company that replaces the existing pension plan with its own plan, rolling membership in the old plan and assets in the old trust over into the new plan and trust.

In addition, under subparagraph (b) of paragraph 9, the competent authority of the host State must determine that the recognized plan to which a contribution is made in the other Contracting State generally corresponds to the plan in the host State. Paragraph XII of the Understanding provides that the term "exempt pension trust" includes those arrangements that are treated as exempt pension trusts for purposes of Article 35 (Exempt Pension Trusts). The United States and the Netherlands entered into a competent authority agreement regarding the types of plans in each jurisdiction that will qualify as exempt pension trusts. See Notice 2000-57, 2000-2 C.B 389, 2000-43 I.R.B. 389.

Paragraph 10

Paragraph 10 generally provides U.S. tax treatment for certain contributions by or on behalf of U.S. citizens resident in the Netherlands to exempt pension trusts established in the Netherlands that is comparable to the treatment that would be provided for contributions to U.S. qualified plans. Under subparagraph (a) of paragraph 10, a U.S. citizen resident in the Netherlands may exclude or deduct for U.S. tax purposes certain contributions to an exempt pension trust established in the Netherlands. Qualifying contributions generally include contributions made during the period the U.S. citizen exercises an employment in the Netherlands if expenses of the employment are borne by a Netherlands employer or Netherlands permanent establishment. Similarly, with respect to the U.S. citizen's participation in the Netherlands pension plan, accrued benefits and contributions during that period generally are not treated as taxable income in the United States.

The U.S. tax benefit allowed by paragraph 10, however, is limited to the lesser of the amount of relief allowed for contributions and benefits under a corresponding exempt pension trust established in the Netherlands and, under subparagraph (b), the amount of relief that would be allowed for contributions and benefits under a generally corresponding pension plan established in the United States.

Subparagraph (c) provides that the benefits an individual obtains under paragraph 10 are taken into account when determining that individual's eligibility for benefits under a pension plan established in the United States. Thus, for example, contributions to a Netherlands exempt pension trust may be taken into account in determining whether the individual has exceeded the annual limitation on contributions to an individual retirement account.

Under subparagraph (d), paragraph 10 does not apply to pension contributions and benefits unless the competent authority of the United States has agreed that the pension plan established in the Netherlands generally corresponds to a pension plan established in the United States. As noted above, the United States and the Netherlands have agreed that certain plans in each jurisdiction will qualify as exempt pension trusts. Since paragraph 10 applies only with respect to persons employed by a Netherlands employer or Netherlands permanent establishment, however, the relevant Netherlands plans are those that correspond to employer plans in the United States, and not those that correspond to individual plans.

Paragraph 11

Paragraph 11 provides that the Netherlands will apply the rules of paragraphs 7, 8, 9 and 10 only with respect to U.S. exempt pension trusts that will provide information and surety to the Netherlands with respect to participants in the trust. Under Netherlands law, when a Netherlands resident ceases to be a resident of the Netherlands, the Netherlands makes a "preserved assessment," which means a tax on the amount of the pension attributable to employment in the Netherlands is assessed but not collected. The assessment lasts for 10 years and the employee is required to give surety. If a lump sum distribution or premature withdrawal is made within that time period, the tax is collected.

In addition to the surety provided by the employee who ceases to be a resident, Netherlands pension funds also are required to provide surety or otherwise ensure that the beneficiaries of the plan are not able to avoid taxation by the Netherlands. Under the 1992 Convention, contributions to U.S. pension funds are deductible only if the pension fund corresponds to a Netherlands exempt pension trust. Accordingly, the rules regarding surety already apply to U.S. pension plans to the extent that an employee or employer wishes to deduct pension contributions to the U.S. plan. An explicit rule is needed in the Protocol because Paragraph XII of the Understanding provides that the term "exempt pension trust" includes those arrangements that are treated as exempt pension trusts for purposes of Article 35 (Exempt Pension Trusts). Without the rule in Article 11, U.S. funds arguably no longer would have been subject to the types of surety obligations and information requirements that apply to Netherlands funds.

The Netherlands recognizes that these rules, including in particular those that require surety from both the employee and the pension fund may be burdensome, however, and therefore has agreed, in Paragraph XIII of the Understanding, that the competent authorities should work together to develop less burdensome methods of complying with these rules.

Relation to other Articles

Subparagraph (c) of Article 6 of the Protocol adds paragraphs 7, 8 and 10 of Article 19 as exceptions to the saving clause of paragraph 1 of Article 24 (Basis of Taxation). Accordingly, a U.S. resident who is a beneficiary of a Netherlands pension plan will not be subject to tax in the United States on the earnings and accretions of a Netherlands exempt pension trust with respect to that U.S. resident. In addition, a U.S. resident may claim the benefits of paragraph 8 if he meets its conditions. Finally, U.S. citizens who are residents of the Netherlands will receive the benefits provided by paragraph 10 with respect to contributions made to exempt pension trusts established in the Netherlands.

Article 6

Article 6 of the Protocol makes several changes to Article 24 (Basis of Taxation) of the Convention.

The changes provided in paragraphs (a) and (b) modify paragraph 1 of Article 24 of the Convention which permits the United States to continue to tax as U.S. citizens former citizens (other than Netherlands nationals) whose loss of citizenship had as one of its principal purposes the avoidance of tax. To reflect 1996 amendments to U.S. tax law in this area, the Protocol extends this treatment to former long term residents whose loss of such status had as one of its principal purposes the avoidance of tax.

Section 877 of the Code applies to former citizens and long-term residents of the United States whose loss of citizenship or long-term resident status had as one of its principal purposes the avoidance of tax. Under section 877, the United States generally treats an individual as having a principal purpose to avoid tax if either of the following criteria exceed established thresholds: (a) the average annual net income tax of such individual for the period of 5 taxable years ending before the date of the loss of status, or (b) the net worth of such individual as of the date of the loss of status. The thresholds are adjusted annually for inflation. Section 877(c) provides certain exceptions to these presumptions of tax avoidance. The United States defines "long-term resident" as an individual (other than a U.S. citizen) who is a lawful permanent resident of the United States in at least 8 of the prior 15 taxable years. An individual is not treated as a lawful permanent resident for any taxable year if such individual is treated as a resident of a foreign country under the provisions of a tax treaty between the United States and the foreign country and the individual does not waive the benefits of such treaty applicable to residents of the foreign country.

The changes made by paragraph (c) and paragraph (d) are discussed above in connection with Article 5 of the Protocol and Article 3 of the Protocol, respectively.

As noted in the Technical Explanation of Article 2 of the Protocol, paragraph (e) of Article 6 updates the Convention's rules regarding fiscally transparent entities by adding a new paragraph 4 to Article 24 of the Convention. In general, paragraph 4 relates to entities that are not subject to tax at the entity level, such as partnerships and certain estates and trusts, as distinct from entities that are subject to tax, but with respect to which tax may be relieved under an integrated system. This paragraph applies to any resident of a Contracting State who is entitled to income derived through an entity that is treated as fiscally transparent under the laws of either Contracting State. Entities falling under this description in the United States include partnerships, common investment trusts under section 584 and grantor trusts. This paragraph also applies to U.S. limited liability companies ("LLCs") that are treated as partnerships for U.S. tax purposes.

Under paragraph 4, an item of income, profit or gain derived by such a fiscally transparent entity will be considered to be derived by a resident of a Contracting State if a resident is treated under the taxation laws of that State as deriving the item of income. For example, if a Netherlands company pays interest to an entity that is treated as fiscally transparent for U.S. tax purposes, the interest will be considered derived by a resident of the United States only to the extent that the taxation laws of the United States treats one or more U.S. residents (whose status as U.S. residents is determined, for this purpose, under U.S. tax law) as deriving the interest for U.S. tax purposes. In the case of a partnership, the persons who are, under U.S. tax laws, treated as partners of the entity would normally be the persons whom the U.S. tax laws would treat as deriving the interest income through the partnership. Also, it follows that persons whom the United States treats as partners but who are not U.S. residents for U.S. tax purposes may not claim a benefit for the interest paid to the entity under the Convention, because they are not residents of the United States for purposes of claiming this treaty benefit. (If, however, the country in which they are treated as resident for tax purposes, as determined under the laws of that country, has an income tax convention with the Netherlands, they may be entitled to claim a benefit under that convention.) In contrast, if, for example, an entity is organized under U.S. laws and is classified as a corporation for U.S. tax purposes, interest paid by a Netherlands company to the U.S. entity will be considered derived by a resident of the United States since the U.S. corporation is treated under U.S. taxation laws as a resident of the United States and as deriving the income.

The same result obtains even if the entity is viewed differently under the tax laws of the Netherlands (*e.g.*, as not fiscally transparent in the first example above where the entity is treated as a partnership for U.S. tax purposes). Similarly, the characterization of the entity in a third country is also irrelevant, even if the entity is organized in that third country. The results follow regardless of whether the entity is disregarded as a separate entity under the laws of one jurisdiction but not the other, such as a single owner entity that is viewed as a branch for U.S. tax purposes and as a corporation for Netherlands tax purposes. These results also obtain regardless of where the entity is organized (*i.e.*, in the United States, in the Netherlands, or, as noted above, in a third country).

For example, income from U.S. sources received by an entity organized under the laws of the United States, which is treated for Netherlands tax purposes as a corporation and is owned by a Netherlands shareholder who is a Netherlands resident for Netherlands tax purposes, is not considered derived by the shareholder of that corporation even if, under the tax laws of the United States, the entity is treated as fiscally transparent.

These principles also apply to trusts to the extent that they are fiscally transparent in either Contracting State. For example, if X, a resident of the Netherlands, creates a revocable trust in the United States and names persons resident in a third country as the beneficiaries of the trust, X would be treated under U.S. law as the beneficial owner of income derived from the United States. In that case, the trust's income would be regarded as being derived by a resident of the Netherlands only to the extent that the laws of the Netherlands treat X as deriving the income for Netherlands tax purposes.

Under subparagraph (b) of Paragraph XIV of the Understanding, the competent authorities may agree to deviate from this general principle in cases where the characterization by the residence country is irrelevant to the taxation of the resident of that country. The Understanding provides the example of an exempt pension trust that is a resident of the Netherlands and that invests in the United States through a U.S. LLC. In that case, the fact that the United States views the LLC as fiscally transparent and the Netherlands views it as non-transparent is irrelevant to the taxation of the exempt pension trust, which would be exempt on the investment income that it receives through the LLC, even if the Netherlands viewed the LLC as fiscally transparent. The competent authorities reached such an agreement on March 23, 2003, as reported in Announcement 2003-21, 2003-17 I.R.B. 846.

Paragraph 4 is not an exception to the saving clause of paragraph 1. Accordingly, as confirmed by subparagraph (a) of Paragraph XIV of the Understanding, paragraph 4 does not prevent a Contracting State from taxing an entity that is treated as a resident of that State under its tax law. For example, if a U.S. LLC with Netherlands members elects to be taxed as a corporation for U.S. tax purposes, the United States will tax that LLC on its worldwide income on a net basis, and will impose withholding tax, at the rate provided in Article 10, on dividends paid by the LLC, without regard to whether the Netherlands views the LLC as fiscally transparent.

Article 7

Article 7 of the Protocol replaces Article 26 (Limitation on Benefits) of the Convention.

Structure of the Article

Article 26 follows the form used in other recent U.S. income tax treaties. Paragraph 1 states the general rule that a resident of a Contracting State is entitled to benefits otherwise accorded to residents only to the extent that the resident satisfies the requirements of the Article and any other specified conditions for the obtaining of such benefits. Paragraph 2 lists a series of attributes of a resident of a Contracting State, any one of which suffices to make such resident a "qualified person" and thus entitled to all the benefits of the Convention. Paragraph 3 provides a so-called "derivative benefits" test under which certain categories of income may qualify for benefits. Paragraph 4 sets forth the active trade or business test, under which a person not entitled to benefits under paragraph 2 may nonetheless be granted benefits with regard to certain types of income. Paragraph 5 provides that a resident of one of the Contracting States is entitled to all the benefits of the Convention if that person functions as a recognized headquarters company for a multinational corporate group. Paragraph 6 provides for limited "derivative benefits" for shipping and air transport income. Paragraph 7 provides that benefits may also be granted if the competent authority of the State from which the benefits are claimed determines that it is appropriate to grant benefits in that case. Paragraph 8 defines the terms used specifically in this Article.

Each of the substantive provisions of Article 26 states that benefits shall be granted only if the resident of a Contracting State satisfies any other specified conditions for claiming benefits. This means, for example, that a publicly-traded company that satisfies the conditions of subparagraph 2(c) will be eligible for the elimination of withholding tax on dividends at source only if it also owns 80 percent or more of the voting power of the paying company and satisfies the 12-month holding period requirement of paragraph 3 of Article 10, and satisfies any other conditions specified in Article 10 or any other articles of the Convention.

Paragraph 1

Paragraph 1 provides that, except as otherwise provided, a resident of a Contracting State will be entitled to all the benefits of the Convention otherwise accorded to residents of a Contracting State only if the resident is a "qualified person" as defined in paragraph 2 of Article 26.

The benefits otherwise accorded to residents under the Convention include all limitations on source-based taxation under Articles 6 through 23 and 27, the treaty-based relief from double taxation provided by Article 25 (Methods of Elimination of Double Taxation), and the protection afforded to residents of a Contracting State under Article 28 (Non-Discrimination). Some provisions do not require that a person be a resident in order to enjoy the benefits of those provisions. Article 29 (Mutual Agreement Procedure) is not limited to residents of the Contracting States, and Article 33 (Diplomatic Agents and Consular Officers) applies to diplomatic agents or consular officials regardless of residence. Article 26 accordingly does not limit the availability of treaty benefits under these provisions.

Article 26 and the anti-abuse provisions of domestic law complement each other, as Article 26 effectively determines whether an entity has a sufficient nexus to the Contracting State to be treated as a resident for treaty purposes, while domestic anti-abuse provisions (*e.g.*, business purpose, substance-over-form, step transaction or conduit principles) determine whether a particular transaction should be recast in accordance with its substance. Thus, internal law principles of the source Contracting State may be applied to identify the beneficial owner of an item of income, and Article 26 then will be applied to the beneficial owner to determine if that person is entitled to the benefits of the Convention with respect to such income.

Paragraph 2

Paragraph 2 has six subparagraphs, each of which describes a category of residents that constitute "qualified persons" and thus are entitled to all benefits of the Convention. It is intended that the provisions of paragraph 2 will be self-executing. Claiming benefits under paragraph 2 does not require advance competent authority ruling or approval. The tax authorities may, of course, on review, determine that the taxpayer has improperly interpreted the paragraph and is not entitled to the benefits claimed.

Individuals -- Subparagraph 2(a)

Subparagraph (a) provides that individual residents of a Contracting State will be entitled to all the benefits of the Convention. If such an individual receives income as a nominee on behalf of a third country resident, benefits may be denied under the applicable articles of the Convention by the requirement that the beneficial owner of the income be a resident of a Contracting State.

Governments -- Subparagraph 2(b)

Subparagraph (b) provides that the Contracting States and any political subdivision or local authority thereof will be entitled to all the benefits of the Convention.

Publicly-Traded Corporations -- Subparagraph 2(c)

Subparagraph (c) applies to two categories of companies: publicly traded companies and subsidiaries of publicly traded companies. A company resident in a Contracting State is entitled to all the benefits of the Convention under clause (i) of subparagraph (c) if the principal class of its shares, and any disproportionate class of shares, is listed on a recognized U.S. or Netherlands stock exchange and is regularly traded on one or more recognized stock exchanges, unless the company has no substantial presence in the State in which it is a resident, as described below.

The term "recognized stock exchange" is defined in subparagraph (a) of paragraph 8. It includes the NASDAQ System and any stock exchange registered with the Securities and Exchange Commission as a national securities exchange for purposes of the Securities Exchange Act of 1934. It also includes the Amsterdam Stock Exchange and any other stock exchange subject to regulation by the Authority for the Financial Markets (or its successor) in the Netherlands. Paragraph XXVII of the Understanding specifies that, for these purposes, certain exchanges that are part of Euronext will be considered to be subject to regulation by the Authority for the Financial Markets. The term also includes the Irish Stock Exchange, the Swiss Stock Exchange, the stock exchanges of Brussels, Frankfurt, Hamburg, Johannesburg, London, Madrid, Milan, Paris, Stockholm, Sydney, Tokyo, Toronto, and Vienna, and any other stock exchange agreed upon by the competent authorities of the Contracting States.

The term "principal class of shares" is defined in subparagraph (b) of paragraph 7. Clause (i) defines the term to mean the ordinary or common shares of the company representing the majority of the aggregate voting power and value of the company. If the company does not have a class of ordinary or common shares representing the majority of the aggregate voting power and value of the company, then the "principal class of shares" is that class or any combination of classes of shares that represents, in the aggregate, a majority of the voting power and value of the company. In addition, clause (ii) of subparagraph (b) defines the term "shares" to include depository receipts for shares or trust certificates for shares.

The term "disproportionate class of shares" is defined in subparagraph (c) of paragraph 8. A company has a disproportionate class of shares if it has outstanding a class of shares which is subject to terms or other arrangements that entitle the holder to a larger portion of the company's income, profit, or gain in the other Contracting State than that to which the holder would be entitled in the absence of such terms or arrangements. Thus, for example, a company resident in the Netherlands meets the test of subparagraph (c) of paragraph 8 if it has outstanding a class of "tracking stock" that pays dividends based upon a formula that approximates the company's return on its assets employed in the United States.

A company whose principal class of stock is publicly traded will nevertheless not qualify for benefits under subparagraph (c) of paragraph 2 if it has a disproportionate class of shares that is not publicly traded. The following example illustrates this result.

Example. DCo is a corporation resident in the Netherlands. DCo has two classes of shares: Common and Preferred. The Common shares are listed and regularly traded on the Amsterdam Stock Exchange. The Preferred shares have no voting rights and are entitled to receive dividends equal in amount to interest payments that DCo receives from unrelated borrowers in the United States. The Preferred shares are owned entirely by a single investor that is a resident of a country with which the United States does not have a tax treaty. The Common shares account for more than 50 percent of the value of DCo and for 100 percent of the voting power. Because the owner of the Preferred shares is entitled to receive payments corresponding to the U.S. source interest income earned by DCo, the Preferred shares are a disproportionate class of shares. Because the Preferred shares are not regularly traded on a recognized stock exchange, DCo will not qualify for benefits under subparagraph (c) of paragraph 2.

A class of shares will be "regularly traded" in a taxable year, under subparagraph (h) of paragraph 8, if the aggregate number of shares of that class traded on one or more recognized exchanges during the twelve months ending on the day before the beginning of that taxable year is at least six percent of the average number of shares outstanding in that class during that twelve-month period. For this purpose, Paragraph XXVII of the Understanding provides that, if a class of shares was not listed on a recognized stock exchange during this twelve-month period, the class of shares will be treated as regularly traded only if the class meets the aggregate trading requirements for the taxable period in which the income arises. Trading on one or more recognized stock exchanges may be aggregated for purposes of meeting the "regularly traded" standard of subparagraph (h). For example, a U.S. company could satisfy the definition of "regularly traded" through trading, in whole or in part, on a recognized stock exchange located in the Netherlands or certain third countries. Authorized but unissued shares are not considered for purposes of subparagraph (h).

The Protocol adds a new requirement to the publicly-traded company test intended to ensure that there is an adequate connection between a public company and its State of residence. A company that is regularly traded on one or more recognized stock exchanges will not qualify for treaty benefits under the publicly-traded company test if it has no "substantial presence" in its country of residence.

There are two components to the "no substantial presence" test. The first component determines whether public trading establishes a sufficient nexus to the State of residence of the company. The second component provides companies with an alternative means for establishing that nexus, by determining whether the company's "primary place of management and control" is in the State of which the company is a resident.

There are two elements to the public trading component of the "no substantial presence" test. The first element compares trading in the State of which the company is not a resident to trading in the company's primary economic zone. For the United States, the primary economic zone is the NAFTA countries and for the Netherlands, the primary economic zone is the European Economic Area and the European Union. Thus, in the case of a Netherlands company, if more trading in its stock takes place on recognized stock exchanges in the United States than on recognized stock exchanges in the EEA and the EU, it will fail the trading component. The second element of the trading component compares trading within the company's primary economic zone with worldwide trading. If the stock of a company is not traded in its primary economic zone at all, or if trading in its primary economic zone constitutes less than 10 percent of total worldwide trading, the company will fail the trading component. Accordingly, a Netherlands company that met the "regularly traded" requirement of the public company test primarily through trading on the Johannesburg, Sydney, Tokyo, or Toronto stock exchanges might fail the trading component.

However, even if a company fails the public trading component of the "no substantial presence" test, it may still qualify for benefits under subparagraph (c) of paragraph 2 if the company's primary place of management and control is in the country of which it is a resident. This test should be distinguished from the "place of effective management" test which is used in the OECD Model and by many other countries to establish residence. In some cases, the place of effective management test has been interpreted to mean the place where the board of directors meets. By contrast, the primary place of management and control test looks to where day-to-day responsibility for the management of the company (and its subsidiaries) is exercised. The company's primary place of management and control will be located in the State in which the company is a resident only if the executive officers and senior management employees exercise day-to-day responsibility for more of the strategic, financial and operational policy decision making for the company (including direct and indirect subsidiaries) in that State than in the other State or any third state, and the staffs that support the management in making those decisions are also based in that State.

Paragraph XXVI of the Understanding provides guidance regarding the persons who are to be considered "executive officers and senior management employees". In most cases, it will not be necessary to look beyond the executive board in the case of a Netherlands company or the executives who are members of the board of directors (the "inside directors") in the case of a U.S. company. That will not always be the case, however, and the Understanding makes clear that the relevant persons may be employees of subsidiaries if they make the strategic, financial and operational policy decisions. Moreover, if there are special voting arrangements that result in certain board members making certain decisions without the participation of other board members, that fact would be taken into account as well.

The following example illustrates the principles of Paragraph XXVI:

Example: NCo is a publicly-traded Netherlands corporation that, along with its subsidiaries, is engaged in the music business. NCo has 50 subsidiaries located in countries around the world, organized under regional holding companies. The local subsidiaries and their regional holding companies are responsible for developing local artists; in most cases, those artists will sell recordings only in their local markets although NCo will choose one or two artists each year to promote globally. The exceptions to this are the U.S. and U.K. subsidiaries of NCo, many of whose artists achieve success worldwide. Because the subsidiaries are primarily responsible for developing their local markets, NCo allows the managers of the subsidiaries substantial autonomy to make significant business decisions, such as the principal artists to sign and how to market and promote them. NCo's substantial Asian operations are managed by employees in its Japanese holding company. Like many Netherlands companies, NCo has both an executive board and a supervisory board. The supervisory board does not participate in decisions before they are made but, pursuant to statute, has oversight responsibilities with respect to the executive board. The members of NCo's executive board include the chief executive officer and chief operating officer of NCo, and the chief executive officers of its U.S. holding company, its U.K. holding company, and its Japanese holding company. On these facts, therefore, the executives most responsible for guiding NCo's global business are members of the executive board. Accordingly, it will not be necessary to look beyond the executive board in applying the management factor.

Paragraph XXVI also includes a special rule for dealing with integrated corporate groups, where staffs located in two different countries support the management of two publicly traded companies. The special rule only applies if the other state in which the staffs are located is in the primary economic zone of the Netherlands and has a tax treaty with the United States that would provide equivalent benefits as the Convention. Thus, at the moment, this rule is limited to integrated corporate groups consisting of a Netherlands publicly traded company and a U.K. publicly traded company and their direct and indirect subsidiaries.

A company resident in a Contracting State is entitled to all the benefits of the Convention under clause (ii) of subparagraph (c) of paragraph 2 if five or fewer publicly traded companies described in clause (i) are the direct or indirect owners of at least 50 percent of the aggregate vote and value of the company's shares (and at least 50 percent of any disproportionate class of shares). If the publicly-traded companies are indirect owners, however, each of the intermediate companies must be a resident of one of the Contracting States. Thus, for example, a Netherlands company, all the shares of which are owned by another Netherlands company, would qualify for benefits under the Convention if the principal class of shares of the Netherlands parent company were listed on the Amsterdam Stock Exchange and regularly traded on the London stock exchange. However, the Netherlands company would not qualify for benefits under clause (ii) if the publicly traded parent company were a resident of Ireland, not of the United States or the Netherlands. Furthermore, if the Netherlands parent indirectly owned the Netherlands company through a chain of subsidiaries, each such subsidiary in the chain, as an intermediate owner, must be a resident of the United States or the Netherlands for the Netherlands company to meet the test in clause (ii).

Exempt Pension Trusts – Subparagraph 2(d)

An exempt pension trust is entitled to all the benefits of the Convention if, as of the close of the end of the prior taxable year, more than 50 percent of the beneficiaries, members or participants of the exempt pension trust are individuals resident in either Contracting State or if the organization sponsoring the pension trust is a qualified person. For purposes of this provision, the term "beneficiaries" should be understood to refer to the persons receiving benefits from the exempt pension trust.

Tax Exempt Organizations -- Subparagraph 2(e)

A tax-exempt organization other than an exempt pension trust is entitled to all the benefits of the Convention, without regard to the residence of its beneficiaries or members. Entities qualifying under this subparagraph are those that generally are exempt from tax in their Contracting State of residence and that are organized and operated exclusively to fulfill religious, charitable, educational, scientific, artistic, cultural, or public purposes.

Ownership/Base Erosion -- Subparagraph 2(f)

Subparagraph 2(f) provides an additional test that applies to any form of legal entity that is a resident of a Contracting State. The test provided in subparagraph (f), the so-called ownership and base erosion test, is a two-part test. Both prongs of the test must be satisfied for the resident to be entitled to benefits under subparagraph 2(f). A company that would be a qualified person under subparagraph 2(c) but for the fact that it has no substantial presence in its State of residence may not qualify for benefits under subparagraph 2(f).

The ownership prong of the test, under clause (i), requires that 50 percent or more of the aggregate voting power and value of the person (and 50 percent or more of any disproportionate class of shares) be owned directly or indirectly on at least half the days of the person's taxable year by persons who are themselves qualified persons under certain other tests of paragraph 2 — subparagraphs (a), (b), (d) or (e), or clause (i) of subparagraph (c).

Trusts may be entitled to benefits under this provision if they are treated as residents under Article 4 (Resident) and they otherwise satisfy the requirements of this subparagraph. For purposes of this subparagraph, the beneficial interests in a trust will be considered to be owned by its beneficiaries in proportion to each beneficiary's actuarial interest in the trust. The interest of a remainder beneficiary will be equal to 100 percent less the aggregate percentages held by income beneficiaries. A beneficiary's interest in a trust will not be considered to be owned by a person entitled to benefits under the other provisions of paragraph 2 if it is not possible to determine the beneficiary's actuarial interest. Consequently, if it is not possible to determine the actuarial interest of the beneficiaries in a trust, the ownership test under clause i) cannot be satisfied, unless all possible beneficiaries are persons entitled to benefits under the other subparagraphs of paragraph 2.

The base erosion prong of clause (ii) of subparagraph (f) is not satisfied with respect to a person if 50 percent or more of the person's gross income for the taxable year is paid or accrued to a person or persons who are not residents of either Contracting State, in the form of payments deductible for tax purposes in the payer's State of residence. For this purpose, Paragraph XV of the Understanding states that the term "gross income" means total revenues derived by a resident of a Contracting State from its principal operations, less the direct costs of obtaining such revenues. In the case of the United States, the term "gross income" has the same meaning as such term in section 61 of the Code and the regulations thereunder.

To the extent they are deductible from the taxable base, trust distributions are deductible payments. However, depreciation and amortization deductions, which do not represent payments or accruals to other persons, are disregarded for this purpose. Deductible payments also do not include arm's length payments in the ordinary course of business for services or tangible property or with respect to financial obligations to banks that are residents of either Contracting State or that have a permanent establishment in either Contracting State to which the payment is attributable.

Paragraph 3

Paragraph 3 sets forth a derivative benefits test that is potentially applicable to all treaty benefits, although the test is applied to individual items of income. In general, a derivative benefits test entitles the resident of a Contracting State to treaty benefits if the owner of the resident would have been entitled to the same benefit had the income in question flowed directly to that owner. To qualify under this paragraph, the company must meet an ownership test and a base erosion test.

Subparagraph (a) sets forth the ownership test. Under this test, seven or fewer equivalent beneficiaries must own shares representing at least 95 percent of the aggregate voting power and value of the company. Ownership may be direct or indirect. The term "equivalent beneficiary" is defined in subparagraph (f) of paragraph 8. This definition may be met in two alternative ways, the first of which has two requirements.

Under the first alternative, a person may be an equivalent beneficiary because it is entitled to equivalent benefits under a treaty between the country of source and the country in which the person is a resident. This alternative has two requirements.

The first requirement is that the person must be a resident of a Member State of the European Community, a European Economic Area state, or a party to the North American Free Trade Agreement (collectively, "qualifying States").

The second requirement of the definition of "equivalent beneficiary" is that the person must be entitled to equivalent benefits under an applicable treaty. To satisfy the second requirement, the person must be entitled to all the benefits of a comprehensive treaty between the Contracting State from which benefits of the Convention are claimed and a qualifying State under provisions that are analogous to the rules in Paragraph 2 regarding individuals, qualified governmental entities, publicly-traded companies or entities, and tax-exempt organizations. Moreover, if the treaty in question does not have a comprehensive limitation on benefits article, this requirement only is met if the person would be a "qualified person" under the tests in Paragraph 2 applicable to individuals, qualified governmental entities, publicly-traded companies or entities, and tax-exempt organizations.

In order to satisfy the additional requirement necessary to qualify as an "equivalent beneficiary" under paragraph 8(f)(i)(B) with respect to dividends, interest, royalties or branch tax, the person must be entitled to a rate of withholding tax that is at least as low as the withholding tax rate that would apply under the Convention to such income. Thus, the rates to be compared are: (1) the rate of withholding tax that the source State would have imposed if a qualified resident of the other Contracting State was the beneficial owner of the income; and (2) the rate of withholding tax that the source State would have imposed if the third State resident received the income directly from the source State. For example, USCo is a wholly owned subsidiary of DCo, a company resident in the Netherlands. DCo is wholly owned by ICo, a corporation resident in Italy. Assuming DCo satisfies the requirements of paragraph 3 of Article 10 (Dividends), DCo would be eligible for the elimination of dividend withholding tax. The dividend withholding tax rate in the treaty between the United States and Italy is 5 percent. Thus, if ICo received the dividend directly from USCo, ICo would have been subject to a 5 percent rate of withholding tax on the dividend. Because ICo would not be entitled to a rate of withholding tax that is at least as low as the rate that would apply under the Convention to such income (*i.e.*, zero), ICo is not an equivalent beneficiary within the meaning of paragraph 8(f)(i) of Article 26 with respect to the elimination of withholding tax on dividends.

Subparagraph 8(g) provides a special rule to take account of the fact that withholding taxes on many inter-company dividends, interest and royalties are exempt within the European Union by reason of various EU directives, rather than by tax treaty. If a U.S. company receives such payments from a Netherlands company, and that U.S. company is owned by a company resident in a Member State of the European Union that would have qualified for an exemption from withholding tax if it had received the income directly, the parent company will be treated as an equivalent beneficiary. This rule is necessary because many EU member countries have not re-negotiated their tax treaties to reflect the rates applicable under the directives.

Paragraph XVII of the Understanding illustrates the "all the benefits" requirement. The requirement that a person be entitled to "all the benefits" of a comprehensive tax treaty eliminates those persons that qualify for benefits with respect to only certain types of income. Accordingly, the fact that a French parent of a Netherlands company is engaged in the active conduct of a trade or business in France and therefore would be entitled to the benefits of the U.S.-France treaty if it received dividends directly is not sufficient for purposes of this paragraph. Further, the French company cannot be an equivalent beneficiary if it qualifies for benefits only with respect to certain income as a result of a "derivative benefits" provision in the U.S.-France treaty. However, it would be possible to look through the French company to its parent company to determine whether the parent company is an equivalent beneficiary.

The second alternative for satisfying the "equivalent beneficiary" test is available only to residents of one of the two Contracting States. U.S. or Netherlands residents who are qualified persons by reason of subparagraphs a), b), c)(i), d), or e) of paragraph 2 are equivalent beneficiaries for purposes of the relevant tests in Article 26. Thus, a Netherlands individual will be an equivalent beneficiary without regard to whether the individual would have been entitled to receive the same benefits if it received the income directly. A resident of a third country cannot be a "qualified person" by reason of those paragraphs or any other rule of the treaty, and therefore do not qualify as equivalent beneficiaries under this alternative. Thus, a resident of a third country can be an equivalent beneficiary only if it would have been entitled to equivalent benefits had it received the income directly.

The second alternative was included in order to clarify that ownership by certain residents of a Contracting State would not disqualify a U.S. or Netherlands company under this paragraph. Thus, for example, if 90 percent of a Netherlands company is owned by five companies that are resident in member states of the European Union who satisfy the requirements of clause (i), and 10 percent of the Netherlands company is owned by a U.S. or Netherlands individual, then the Netherlands company still can satisfy the requirements of subparagraph (a) of paragraph 3.

Subparagraph (b) sets forth the base erosion test. A company meets this base erosion test if less than 50 percent of its gross income for the taxable period is paid or accrued, directly or indirectly, to a person or persons who are not equivalent beneficiaries in the form of payments deductible for tax purposes in company's State of residence. This test is the same as the base erosion test in clause (ii) of subparagraph (f) of paragraph 2, except that deductible payments made to equivalent beneficiaries, rather than amounts paid to residents of a Contracting State, are not counted against a company for purposes of determining whether the company exceeded the 50 percent limit.

As in the case of base erosion test in subparagraph (f) of paragraph 2, deductible payments in subparagraph (b) of paragraph 3 also do not include arm's length payments in the ordinary course of business for services or tangible property or with respect to financial obligations to banks that are residents of either Contracting State or that have a permanent establishment in either Contracting State to which the payment is attributable.

Under the 1992 Convention, the derivative benefits provision had somewhat different requirements. The test required that 30 percent of the shares of the company claiming benefits be owned by Netherlands residents, but only 70 percent of the shares had to be owned by equivalent beneficiaries (including Netherlands residents). It is possible that some companies would qualify for benefits under the prior test, but not under the provisions of paragraph 3, and vice versa. Since satisfaction of the prior test demonstrates a close connection to the Netherlands, it remains a valid objective test. Accordingly, subparagraph (a) of Paragraph XXIV of the Understanding provides that a company will be granted the benefits of the Convention pursuant to the competent authority discretion provision in cases where more than 30 percent of vote and value of the company's shares are owned by residents of a Contracting State that are described in subparagraph 8(f)(ii) and more than 70 percent of the shares (and at least 50 percent of any disproportionate class of shares) is owned by seven or fewer equivalent beneficiaries, provided that the base erosion test has been met.

Paragraph 4

Paragraph 4 sets forth a test under which a resident of a Contracting State that is not a "qualified person" under paragraph 2 may receive treaty benefits with respect to certain items of income that are connected to an active trade or business conducted in its State of residence.

Subparagraph (a) sets forth the general rule that a resident of a Contracting State engaged in the active conduct of a trade or business in that State may obtain the benefits of the Convention with respect to an item of income, profit, or gain derived in the other Contracting State. The item of income, profit, or gain, however, must be derived in connection with or incidental to that trade or business.

The term "trade or business" is not defined in the Convention. Pursuant to paragraph 2 of Article 3 (General Definitions), when determining whether a resident of the Netherlands is entitled to the benefits of the Convention under paragraph 4 of this Article with respect to an item of income derived from sources within the United States, the United States will ascribe to this term the meaning that it has under the law of the United States. Accordingly, the U.S. competent authority will refer to the regulations issued under section 367(a) for the definition of the term "trade or business." In general, therefore, a trade or business will be considered to be a specific unified group of activities that constitute or could constitute an independent economic enterprise carried on for profit. Furthermore, a corporation generally will be considered to carry on a trade or business only if the officers and employees of the corporation conduct substantial managerial and operational activities.

The business of making or managing investments for the resident's own account will be considered to be a trade or business only when part of banking, insurance or securities activities conducted by a bank, an insurance company, or a registered securities dealer. Such activities conducted by a person other than a bank, insurance company or registered securities dealer will not be considered to be the conduct of an active trade or business, nor would they be considered to be the conduct of an active trade or business if conducted by a bank, insurance company or registered securities dealer but not as part of the company's banking, insurance or dealer business.

For this purpose, Paragraph XX of the Understanding states that a bank will be considered to be engaged in the active conduct of a trade or business only if it regularly accepts deposits from the public and makes loans to the public. Furthermore, an insurance company only is engaged in the active conduct of an insurance business if its gross income consists primarily of insurance or reinsurance premiums and investment income attributable to such premiums.

Because a headquarters operation is in the business of managing investments, a company that functions solely as a headquarters company will not be considered to be engaged in an active trade or business for purposes of subparagraph (a). It may, however, qualify for benefits if it meets the requirements of paragraph 5.

Paragraph XIX of the Understanding provides that an item of income is derived in connection with a trade or business if the income-producing activity in the State of source is a line of business that "forms a part of" or is "complementary" to the trade or business conducted in the State of residence by the income recipient.

A business activity generally will be considered to form part of a business activity conducted in the State of source if the two activities involve the design, manufacture or sale of the same products or type of products, or the provision of similar services. The notes clarify that the line of business in the State of residence may be upstream, downstream, or parallel to the activity conducted in the State of source. Thus, the line of business may provide inputs for a manufacturing process that occurs in the State of source, may sell the output of that manufacturing process, or simply may sell the same sorts of products that are being sold by the trade or business carried on in the State of source.

Example 1. USCo is a corporation resident in the United States. USCo is engaged in an active manufacturing business in the United States. USCo owns 100 percent of the shares of DCo, a company resident in the Netherlands. DCo distributes USCo products in the Netherlands. Because the business activities conducted by the two corporations involve the same products, DCo's distribution business is considered to form a part of USCo's manufacturing business.

Example 2. The facts are the same as in Example 1, except that USCo does not manufacture. Rather, USCo operates a large research and development facility in the

United States that licenses intellectual property to affiliates worldwide, including DCo. DCo and other USCo affiliates then manufacture and market the USCo-designed products in their respective markets. Because the activities conducted by DCo and USCo involve the same product lines, these activities are considered to form a part of the same trade or business.

For two activities to be considered to be "complementary," the activities need not relate to the same types of products or services, but they should be part of the same overall industry and be related in the sense that the success or failure of one activity will tend to result in success or failure for the other. Where more than one trade or business is conducted in the State of source and only one of the trades or businesses forms a part of or is complementary to a trade or business conducted in the State of residence, it is necessary to identify the trade or business to which an item of income is attributable. Royalties generally will be considered to be derived in connection with the trade or business to which the underlying intangible property is attributable. Dividends will be deemed to be derived first out of earnings and profits of the treaty-benefited trade or business, and then out of other earnings and profits. Interest income may be allocated under any reasonable method consistently applied. A method that conforms to U.S. principles for expense allocation will be considered a reasonable method.

Example 3. Americair is a corporation resident in the United States that operates an international airline. DSub is a wholly-owned subsidiary of Americair resident in the Netherlands. DSub operates a chain of hotels in the Netherlands that are located near airports served by Americair flights. Americair frequently sells tour packages that include air travel to the Netherlands and lodging at DSub hotels. Although both companies are engaged in the active conduct of a trade or business, the businesses of operating a chain of hotels and operating an airline are distinct trades or businesses. Therefore DSub's business does not form a part of Americair's business. However, DSub's business is considered to be complementary to Americair's business because they are part of the same overall industry (travel), and the links between their operations tend to make them interdependent.

Example 4. The facts are the same as in Example 3, except that DSub owns an office building in the Netherlands instead of a hotel chain. No part of Americair's business is conducted through the office building. DSub's business is not considered to form a part of or to be complementary to Americair's business. They are engaged in distinct trades or businesses in separate industries, and there is no economic dependence between the two operations.

Example 5. USFlower is a company resident in the United States. USFlower produces and sells flowers in the United States and other countries. USFlower owns all the shares of DHolding, a corporation resident in the Netherlands. DHolding is a holding company that is not engaged in a trade or business. DHolding owns all the shares of three corporations that are resident in the Netherlands: DFlower, DLawn, and DFish. DFlower distributes USFlower flowers under the USFlower trademark in the Netherlands. DLawn markets a line of lawn care products in the Netherlands under the USFlower trademark.

In addition to being sold under the same trademark, DLawn and DFlower products are sold in the same stores and sales of each company's products tend to generate increased sales of the other's products. DFish imports fish from the United States and distributes it to fish wholesalers in the Netherlands. For purposes of paragraph 4, the business of DFlower forms a part of the business of USFlower, the business of DLawn is complementary to the business of USFlower, and the business of DFish is neither part of nor complementary to that of USFlower.

Paragraph XIX of the Understanding also provides that an item of income derived from the State of source is "incidental to" the trade or business carried on in the State of residence if production of the item facilitates the conduct of the trade or business in the State of residence. An example of incidental income is the temporary investment of working capital of a person in the State of residence in securities issued by persons in the State of source.

Subparagraph (b) of paragraph 4 states a further condition to the general rule in subparagraph (a) in cases where the trade or business generating the item of income in question is carried on either by the person deriving the income or by any associated enterprises. Subparagraph (b) states that the trade or business carried on in the State of residence, under these circumstances, must be substantial in relation to the activity in the State of source. Paragraph XXII of the Understanding elaborates on the purpose and application of the substantiality requirement. The requirement is intended to prevent a narrow case of treaty-shopping abuses in which a company attempts to qualify for benefits by engaging in de minimis connected business activities in the treaty country in which it is resident (*i.e.*, activities that have little economic cost or effect with respect to the company business as a whole).

The determination of substantiality is made based upon all the facts and circumstances and takes into account the comparative sizes of the trades or businesses in each Contracting State (measured by reference to asset values, income and payroll expenses), the nature of the activities performed in each Contracting State, and the relative contributions made to that trade or business in each Contracting State. In any case, in making each determination or comparison, due regard will be given to the relative sizes of the U.S. and Netherlands economies.

In addition to this subjective rule, Paragraph XXII of the Understanding provides a safe harbor under which the trade or business of the income recipient may be deemed to be substantial based on three ratios that compare the size of the recipient's activities to those conducted in the other State with respect to the preceding taxable year, or the average of the preceding three years. The three ratios compare: (i) the value of the assets in the recipient's State to the assets used in the other State; (ii) the gross income derived in the recipient's State to the gross income derived in the other State; and (iii) the payroll expense in the recipient's State to the payroll expense in the other State. The average of the three ratios must exceed 10 percent, and each individual ratio must equal at least 7.5 percent. For purposes of this test, if the income recipient owns, directly or indirectly, less than 100 percent of the activity conducted in either State, only its proportionate share of the activity will be taken into account.

The determination in subparagraph (b) also is made separately for each item of income derived from the State of source. It therefore is possible that a person would be entitled to the benefits of the Convention with respect to one item of income but not with respect to another. If a resident of a Contracting State is entitled to treaty benefits with respect to a particular item of income under paragraph 4, the resident is entitled to all benefits of the Convention insofar as they affect the taxation of that item of income in the State of source.

The application of the substantiality test only to income from related parties focuses only on potential abuse cases, and does not hamper certain other kinds of non-abusive activities, even though the income recipient resident in a Contracting State may be very small in relation to the entity generating income in the other Contracting State. For example, if a small U.S. research firm develops a process that it license to a very large, unrelated, Netherlands pharmaceutical manufacturer, the size of the U.S. research firm would not have to be tested against the size of the Netherlands manufacturer. Similarly, a small U.S. bank that makes a loan to a very large unrelated Netherlands business would not have to pass a substantiality test to receive treaty benefits under Paragraph 4.

Subparagraph (c) of paragraph 4 provides special rules for determining whether a resident of a Contracting State is engaged in the active conduct of a trade or business within the meaning of subparagraph (a). Subparagraph (c) attributes the activities of a partnership to each of its partners. Subparagraph (c) also attributes to a person activities conducted by persons "connected" to such person. A person ("X") is connected to another person ("Y") if X possesses 50 percent or more of the beneficial interest in Y (or if Y possesses 50 percent or more of the beneficial interest in X). For this purpose, X is connected to a company if X owns shares representing fifty percent or more of the aggregate voting power and value of the company or fifty percent or more of the beneficial equity interest in the company. X also is connected to Y if a third person possesses fifty percent or more of the beneficial interest in both X and Y. For this purpose, if X or Y is a company, the threshold relationship with respect to such company or companies is fifty percent or more of the aggregate voting power and value or fifty percent or more of the beneficial equity interest. Finally, X is connected to Y if, based upon all the facts and circumstances, X controls Y, Y controls X, or X and Y are controlled by the same person or persons.

Paragraph 5

Paragraph 5 provides that a resident of one of the Contracting States is entitled to all the benefits of the Convention if that person functions as a recognized headquarters company for a multinational corporate group. For this purpose, the multinational corporate group includes all corporations that the headquarters company supervises and excludes affiliated corporations not supervised by the headquarters company. The headquarters company does not have to own shares in the companies that it supervises. In order to be considered a headquarters company, the person must meet several requirements that are enumerated in Paragraph 5. These requirements are discussed below.

Overall Supervision and Administration

Subparagraph (a) provides that the person must provide a substantial portion of the overall supervision and administration of the group. This activity may include group financing, but group financing may not be the principal activity of the person functioning as the headquarters company. A person only will be considered to engage in supervision and administration if it engages in a number of the following activities: group financing, pricing, marketing, internal auditing, internal communications, and management. Other activities also could be part of the function of supervision and administration.

In determining whether a "substantial portion" of the overall supervision and administration of the group is provided by the headquarters company, its headquarters-related activities must be substantial in relation to the same activities for the same group performed by other entities.

Subparagraph (a) does not require that the group that is supervised include persons in the other State. However, it is anticipated that in most cases the group will include such persons, due to the requirement discussed below that the income derived by the headquarters company be derived in connection with or be incidental to an active trade or business supervised by the headquarters company.

Active Trade or Business

Subparagraph (b) is the first of several requirements intended to ensure that the relevant group is truly "multinational." This sub-paragraph provides that the corporate group supervised by the headquarters company must consist of corporations resident in, and engaged in active trades or businesses in, at least five countries. Furthermore, at least five countries must contribute substantially to the income generated by the group, as the rule requires that the business activities carried on in each of the five countries (or groupings of countries) generate at least 10 percent of the gross income of the group. For purposes of the 10 percent gross income requirement, the income from multiple countries may be aggregated, as long as there are at least five individual countries or groupings that each satisfy the 10 percent requirement. If the gross income requirement under this clause is not met for a taxable year, the taxpayer may satisfy this requirement by averaging the ratios for the four years preceding the taxable year.

Example 1. DHQ is a corporation resident in the Netherlands. DHQ functions as a headquarters company for a group of companies. These companies are resident in the United States, Canada, New Zealand, the United Kingdom, Malaysia, the Philippines, Singapore, and Indonesia. The gross income generated by each of these companies for 2004 and 2005 is as follows:

Country	2004	2005
United States	$40	$45
Canada	$25	$15
New Zealand	$10	$20
United Kingdom	$30	$35
Malaysia	$10	$12
Philippines	$ 7	$10
Singapore	$10	$ 8
Indonesia	$ 5	$10
	$137	$155

For 2004, 10 percent of the gross income of this group is equal to $13.70. Only the United States, Canada, and the United Kingdom satisfy this requirement for that year. The other companies in the group may be aggregated to meet this requirement. Because New Zealand and Malaysia have a total gross income of $20, and the Philippines, Singapore, and Indonesia have a total gross income of $22, these two groupings of countries may be treated as the fourth and fifth members of the group for purposes of clause (2)(h)(ii).

In the following year, 10 percent of the gross income is $15.50. Only the United States, New Zealand, and the United Kingdom satisfy this requirement. Because Canada and Malaysia have a total gross income of $27, and the Philippines, Singapore, and Indonesia have a total gross income of $28, these two groupings of countries may be treated as the fourth and fifth members of the group for purposes of clause (2)(h)(ii). The fact that Canada replaced New Zealand in a group not relevant for this purpose. The composition of the grouping may change from year to year.

Single Country Limitation

Subparagraph (c) provides that the business activities carried on in any one country other than the headquarters company's state of residence must generate less than 50 percent of the gross income of the group. If the gross income requirement under this clause is not met for a taxable year, the taxpayer may satisfy this requirement by averaging the ratios for the four years preceding the taxable year. The following example illustrates the application of this subparagraph.

Example. DHQ is a corporation resident in the Netherlands. DHQ functions as a headquarters company for a group of companies. DHQ derives dividend income from a United States subsidiary in the 2004 taxable year. The state of residence of each of these companies, the situs of their activities and the amounts of gross income attributable to each for the years 2004 through 2008 are set forth below.

Company	Situs	2008	2007	2006	2005	2004
United States	U.S.	$100	$100	$ 95	$ 90	$ 85

35

United States	Mexico	10	8	5	0	0
United States	Canada	20	18	16	15	12
United Kingdom	U.K	30	32	30	28	27
New Zealand	N.Z.	40	42	38	36	35
Japan	Japan	35	32	30	30	28
Singapore	Singapore	25	25	24	22	20
		$260	$257	$238	$221	$207

Because the United States' total gross income of $130 in 2008 is not less than 50 percent of the gross income of the group, clause (2)(h)(iii) is not satisfied with respect to dividends derived in 2008. However, the United States' average gross income for the preceding four years may be used in lieu of the preceding year's average. The United States' average gross income for the years 2004-07 is $111.00 ($444/4). The group's total average gross income for these years is $230.75 ($923/4). Because $111.00 represents 48.1 percent of the group's average gross income for the years 2004 through 2007, the requirement under subparagraph (c) is satisfied.

Other State Gross Income Limitation

Subparagraph (d) provides that no more than 25 percent of the headquarters company's gross income may be derived from the other Contracting State. Thus, if the headquarters company's gross income for the taxable year is $200, no more than $50 of this amount may be derived from the other Contracting State. If the gross income requirement under this clause is not met for a taxable year, the taxpayer may satisfy this requirement by averaging the ratios for the four years preceding the taxable year.

Independent Discretionary Authority

Subparagraph (e) requires that the headquarters company have and exercise independent discretionary authority to carry out the functions referred to in subparagraph (a). Thus, if the headquarters company was nominally responsible for group financing, pricing, marketing and other management functions, but merely implemented instructions received from another entity, the headquarters company would not be considered to have and exercise independent discretionary authority with respect to these functions. This determination is made individually for each function. For instance, a headquarters company could be nominally responsible for group financing, pricing, marketing and internal auditing functions, but another entity could be actually directing the headquarters company as to the group financing function. In such a case, the headquarters company would not be deemed to have independent discretionary authority for group financing, but it might have such authority for the other functions. Functions for which the headquarters company does not have and exercise independent discretionary authority are considered to be conducted by an entity other than the headquarters company for purposes of subparagraph (a).

Income Taxation Rules

Subparagraph (f) requires that the headquarters company be subject to the generally applicable income taxation rules in its country of residence. This reference should be understood to mean that the company must be subject to the income taxation rules to which a company engaged in the active conduct of a trade or business would be subject. Thus, if one of the Contracting States has or introduces special taxation legislation that impose a lower rate of income tax on headquarters companies than is imposed on companies engaged in the active conduct of a trade or business, or provides for an artificially low taxable base for such companies, a headquarters company subject to these rules is not entitled to the benefits of the Convention under Paragraph 5.

In Connection With or Incidental to Trade or Business

Subparagraph (g) requires that the income derived in the other Contracting State be derived in connection with or be incidental to the active business activities referred to in subparagraph (b). This determination is made under the principles set forth in paragraph 4. For instance, if a Netherlands company that satisfied the other requirements in Paragraph 5 acted as a headquarters company for a group that included a United States corporation, and the group was engaged in the design and manufacture of computer software, but the U.S. company was also engaged in the design and manufacture of photocopying machines, the income that the Netherlands company derived from the United States would have to be derived in connection with or be incidental to the income generated by the computer business in order to be entitled to the benefits of the Convention under Paragraph 5. Interest income received from the U.S. company also would be entitled to the benefits of the Convention under this paragraph as long as the interest was attributable to a trade or business supervised by the headquarters company. Interest income derived from an unrelated party would normally not, however, satisfy the requirements of this clause.

Paragraph 6

Paragraph 6 provides that a resident of one of the States that derives income from the other State described in Article 8 (Shipping and Air Transport) and that is not entitled to the benefits of the Convention under paragraphs 1 through 5, shall nonetheless be entitled to the benefits of the Convention with respect to income described in Article 8 if it meets one of two tests.

First, a resident of one of the States will be entitled to the benefits of the Convention with respect to income described in Article 8 if at least 50 percent of the beneficial interest in the person (in the case of a company, at least 50 percent of the aggregate vote and value of the stock of the company) is owned, directly or indirectly, by qualified persons or individuals who are residents of a third state that grants by law, common agreement, or convention an exemption under similar terms for profits as mentioned in Article 8 to citizens and corporations of the other State. This provision is analogous to the relief provided under Code section 883(c)(1).

Alternatively, a resident of one of the States will be entitled to the benefits of the Convention with respect to income described in Article 8 if at least 50 percent of the beneficial interest in the person (in the case of a company, at least 50 percent of the aggregate vote and value of the stock of the company) is owned directly or indirectly by a company or combination of companies the stock of which is primarily and regularly traded on an established securities market in a third state, provided that the third state grants by law, common agreement or convention an exemption under similar terms for profits as mentioned in Article 8 to citizens and corporations of the other State. This provision is analogous to the relief provided under Code section 883(c)(3). The term "primarily and regularly traded on an established securities market" is not defined in the Convention. In determining whether a resident of the Netherlands is entitled to benefits of the Convention under this paragraph, the United States will apply the principles of Code Section 883(c)(3)(A).

A resident of a Contracting State that derives income from the other State described in Article 8 (Shipping and Air Transport) but that does not meet all the requirements of paragraph 5 will nevertheless qualify for treaty benefits if it meets the requirements of any other test under Article 26 (i.e., the publicly-traded test under paragraph 2(c) or the active trade or business test of paragraph 4).

Paragraph 7

Paragraph 7 provides that a resident of one of the States that is not entitled to the benefits of the Convention as a result of paragraphs 1 through 6 still may be granted benefits under the Convention at the discretion of the competent authority of the State from which benefits are claimed. In making determinations under paragraph 7, that competent authority will take into account as its guideline whether the establishment, acquisition, or maintenance of the person seeking benefits under the Convention, or the conduct of such person's operations, has or had as one of its principal purposes the obtaining of benefits under the Convention. Thus, persons that establish operations in one of the States with a principal purpose of obtaining the benefits of the Convention ordinarily will not be granted relief under paragraph 7.

The competent authority may determine to grant all benefits of the Convention, or it may determine to grant only certain benefits. For instance, it may determine to grant benefits only with respect to a particular item of income in a manner similar to paragraph 3. Further, the competent authority may set time limits on the duration of any relief granted.

For purposes of implementing paragraph 7, a taxpayer will be permitted to present his case to the relevant competent authority for an advance determination based on the facts. In these circumstances, it is also expected that if the competent authority determines that benefits are to be allowed, they will be allowed retroactively to the time of entry into force of the relevant treaty provision or the establishment of the structure in question, whichever is later.

A competent authority is required by paragraph 7 to consult the other competent authority before denying benefits under this paragraph. Subparagraph (b) of Paragraph XXIV of the Understanding includes two provisions intended to ensure that taxpayers receive determinations in a timely manner. First, the competent authorities agree to use reasonable efforts to make a determination pursuant to this paragraph within six months of receiving all of the necessary information from taxpayers. Second, they will meet semi-annually to discuss the status of outstanding cases.

According to paragraph XXVIII of the Understanding, the competent authorities will consider the obligations of the Netherlands by virtue of its membership in the European Communities in making a determination under paragraph 7. In particular, the competent authorities will consider any legal requirements for the facilitation of the free movement of capital and persons, together with the differing internal tax systems, tax incentive regimes and existing tax treaty policies among Member States of the European Communities. As a result, where certain changes in circumstances otherwise might cause a person to cease to be a qualified person under paragraphs 2 and 3 of Article 26, such changes need not result in the denial of benefits.

The changes in circumstances contemplated include, all under ordinary business conditions, a change in the State of residence of a major shareholder of a company; the sale of part of the stock of a Netherlands company to a resident in another Member State of the European Communities; or an expansion of a company's activities in other Member States of the European Communities. So long as the relevant competent authority is satisfied that those changed circumstances are not attributable to tax avoidance motives, they will count as a factor favoring the granting of benefits under paragraph 7, if consistent with existing treaty policies, such as the need for effective exchange of information. See the Technical Explanation to paragraph 3 of Article 10 for a discussion of the factors that the competent authority will consider in making these determinations. A company that wishes the relevant competent authority to take such legal requirements into account must request an advance determination, as described above.

Paragraph 8

Paragraph 8 defines several key terms for purposes of Article 26. Each of the defined terms is discussed in the context in which it is used.

Article 8

Article 8 restates Article 32 (Limitation of Articles 30 and 31) of the Convention to make it consistent with the U.S. Model Tax Convention and international norms regarding information exchange and bank secrecy.

Paragraph 1

Paragraph 1 provides that the obligations undertaken in Articles 30 and 31 to exchange information do not require a Contracting State to carry out administrative measures that are at variance with the laws or administrative practice of either State. Moreover, a Contracting State is not required to supply information not obtainable under the laws or administrative practice of either State, or to disclose trade secrets or other information the disclosure of which would be contrary to public policy. Thus, a requesting State may be denied information from the other State if the information would be obtained pursuant to procedures or measures that are broader than those available in the requesting State. Paragraph XXXIII confirms that the competent authorities will work together to ensure that the information to be provided will be in a form that facilitates its use in judicial proceedings in the requesting State.

Paragraph 2

In paragraph 2, each Contracting State has confirmed that it will obtain and exchange certain information, notwithstanding the provisions of paragraph 1. The information that may be exchanged includes information held by financial institutions, nominees, or persons acting in an agency or fiduciary capacity. The Contracting States may also obtain and exchange information relating to the ownership of legal persons and, as described in paragraph XXXVI of the Understanding, will use all reasonable efforts to do so unless obtaining such information gives rise to disproportionate difficulties.

Paragraph 3

Paragraph 3 confirms that the obligation to provide information held by persons acting in a fiduciary capacity does not extend to information that would reveal confidential communications between a client and an attorney, solicitor or other legal representative, where the client seeks legal advice or produced for the purposes of use in existing or contemplated legal proceedings. In the case of the United States, the scope of the privilege for such confidential communications is coextensive with the attorney-client privilege under U.S. law.

Article 9

Article 9 updates several references in the Convention that have become outdated. Paragraph (a) updates the reference to the Netherlands Mining Act, which consolidated and restated the provisions of the Mining Act of 1810 and the Continental Shelf Mining Act of 1965. Paragraph (b) takes account of the fact that the euro has replaced Netherlands guilders as the currency of the Netherlands.

Article 10

Article 10 contains the rules for bringing the Protocol into force and giving effect to its provisions.

Paragraph 1 provides for the ratification of the Convention by both Contracting States according to their constitutional and statutory requirements. Each State must notify the other as soon as its requirements for ratification have been complied with. The Convention will enter into force on the date of the later of such notifications.

In the United States, the process leading to ratification and entry into force is as follows: Once a protocol or treaty has been signed by authorized representatives of the two Contracting States, the Department of State sends the protocol or treaty to the President who formally transmits it to the Senate for its advice and consent to ratification, which requires approval by two-thirds of the Senators present and voting. Prior to this vote, however, it generally has been the practice of the Senate Committee on Foreign Relations to hold hearings on the protocol or treaty and make a recommendation regarding its approval to the full Senate. Both Government and private sector witnesses may testify at these hearings. After receiving the Senate's advice and consent to ratification, the protocol or treaty is returned to the President for his signature on the ratification document. The President's signature on the document completes the process in the United States.

The date on which a treaty enters into force is not necessarily the date on which its provisions take effect. Paragraph 1 also contains rules that determine when the provisions of the treaty will have effect.

Under subparagraph (a), the provisions of the Protocol relating to taxes withheld at source will have effect with respect to amounts paid or credited on or after the first day of the second month following the date on which the Protocol enters into force. For example, if instruments of ratification are exchanged on April 25 of a given year, the withholding rates specified in paragraphs 2 and 3 of Article 10 (Dividends) as provided in Article 3 would be applicable to any dividends paid or credited on or after June 1 of that year. Similarly, the revised Limitation on Benefits provisions of Article 7 would apply with respect to any payments of interest, royalties or other amounts on which withholding would apply under the Internal Revenue Code if those amounts are paid or credited on or after June 1.

This rule allows the benefits of the withholding reductions to be put into effect as soon as possible, without waiting until the following year. The delay of one to two months is required to allow sufficient time for withholding agents to be informed about the change in withholding rates. If for some reason a withholding agent withholds at a higher rate than that provided by the Convention (perhaps because it was not able to re-program its computers before the payment is made), a beneficial owner of the income that is a resident of the Netherlands may make a claim for refund pursuant to section 1464 of the Code.

For all other taxes, subparagraph (b) specifies that the Protocol will have effect for any taxable period beginning on or after January 1 of the year following entry into force.

As in many recent U.S. treaties, paragraph 2 provides an exception to the general rules of paragraph 1 regarding entry into force. Under paragraph 2, if any person who was entitled to the benefits of the Convention, before modification by the Protocol, would have received greater relief from tax than under the Convention as modified by the Protocol, the Convention as unmodified shall, at the election of any person that was entitled to benefits under the prior Convention, continue to have effect in its entirety for a twelve-month period from the date on which this Convention otherwise would have had effect with respect to such person.

Thus, a taxpayer may elect to extend the benefits of the unmodified Convention for one year from the date on which the relevant provision of the modified Convention would first take effect. During the period in which the election is in effect, the provisions of the unmodified Convention will continue to apply only insofar as they applied before the entry into force of the Protocol. If the grace period is elected, all of the provisions of the Convention as unmodified must be applied for that additional year. The taxpayer may not apply certain, more favorable provisions of the unmodified Convention and, at the same time, apply other, more favorable provisions of modified Convention. The taxpayer must choose one regime or the other.